THE DELIGHT OF WORSHIP

Communicating Through Praise and Worship

LEAH DAVID KOMEN

AuthorHouse™ LLC
1663 Liberty Drive
Bloomington, IN 47403
www.authorhouse.com
Phone: 1-800-839-8640

Published by AuthorHouse 01/08/2014

ISBN: 978-1-4918-8860-5 (sc)
*   978-1-4918-8861-2 (e)*

ACKNOWLEDGEMENT

"A journey of a thousand miles is begun by a single step" a famous Chinese saying. Never has this been true than it is now in my life. This work was as a result of years of meditating on Gods purpose for creating man and continued listening to servants of God as they taught this subject. Reading books on this subject also increased my passion to learn more.

I acknowledge the input of Bishop Mark Kubai Kariuki who is currently the presiding bishop of Deliverance churches Kenya, the late pastor Moses Maina Mwangi and Bishop Paul Muliwa Mwakio for the doors they opened for me to minister in the ministry of Praise and worship. I cannot forget to mention their fatherhood input in the manner in which they allowed me to make mistakes and helped me grow in the area of corporate worship leading. Many thanks go to pastor Dixon Thuo and his wife Mercy who literally mentored me in the worship leadership in their capacity as worship leaders.

I sincerely acknowledge the works of Rev. Stanley and Ann Mwalili who allowed and still do allow uninterrupted praise and worship experience in church. Their passion for praise and Worship infiltrated the whole congregation, and needless to say this part of the service became one of the most cherished by many. Thank you pastor Joe Mbuvi and Joshua Mbugua alongside Pastor Bosire for your incredible contribution to a wonderful worship atmosphere, May the good Lord flourish you in levels you have not known.

To Rev. Albert and Mary Shitakwa, I extent my warm gratitude for not only being a man and woman with hearts for worship, but also the kind that opened opportunity for all. I have found enlarged opportunities not only to share my thoughts on the subject but to actually demonstrate the act of worship. As I would always say, Pasi ! wewe, ni wa maana, meaning your are truly important .

Special appreciation goes to my then music Director Pastor Faith Okuyo now Mrs. Lugonzo who not only proofread my work but also put some input. Faith not many leaders would do what you did in fact they would use the material to either write their own worship books or worse of it all discredit the writer just for a mere fact that they serve under them and so for fear of being outshone allow the spirit of insecurity to take hold of them. Faith there is absolutely no reason why you should not be blessed. You were a selfless leader who never felt insecure but mentored all who cared to be mentored by grace and you sealed it with love. I am grateful to God for you. May the good Lord flourish you.

I wish to single out CITAM Woodley worship team led by Pastor Grace Bukachi who was my music instructor. I learn a lot by observing you mum lead the people of God before God's presence. You are a good example of teamwork spirit and a mother to all. I want you to know pastor B as you are famously referred to, that I appreciate you and keep on keeping on. What an angelic voice you got and a life after God's heart that you have demonstrated. Bless you. I truly love the embracing of all music types in the congregation from hymns, to contemporary Christian music among many.

I specifically want to acknowledge the support of my covenant partner and Husband, Eng. David Komen. Honey you are the best thing that happened to me. You did not only support me financially but morally, emotionally and more so spiritually. I will forever be grateful to God for giving you to me. I enjoy life more as a married woman than I did as a single person. You have indeed been what Dr. Myles Munroe terms as a 'Real man'. The man of God describes a real man as one that not only leads his household in worship but also cultivates his wife. Honey, you are my 'real man', you cultivate me and lead our home in the path of faith. I am so blessed to be married to you. To our sons Emmanuel (13) and Enoch (10), you are the best there is to behold and celebrate; your genuine worship and desire to be Musicians are well appreciated. Our 'Drummer' Emmanuel and 'Guitarist/recorder' player Enoch, we value you so much indeed so proud of the two of you. May your gifts bring you honour even as you worship God who deserves all worship and exaltation. Indeed you are our mighty men of valour.

DEDICATION

This book is dedicated to all children of God who:

1. Want to discover the purpose and power of praise and worship in their lives.

2. Wish to heighten their understanding of the significance of Praise and Worship

3. Are curious to explore the subject of Praise and Worship most importantly.

4. Those who wish to make Praise and Worship of the most high God a lifestyle

Foreword

It is not often that we get a book like THE DELIGHT OF WORSHIP in our hands. For many, worship means different things and at times even within the church no one has an idea what worship is all about. Many of the worship teams lead worship, but without adequate understanding of what worship is all about. This book comes to equip and fill that gap of information that is needed. Indeed the Bible says that by wisdom a house is built, by understanding it is established, by knowledge the rooms are filled with precious treasures. This is what God has enabled the author of this book to do.

Worship needs to be a delight and not just a duty. Worship is directed to God and is not an opportunity of entertainment within the church. Worship has a purpose to bring glory and honor to the living God. Worship is a process and one can grow in it and be a mature worshipper of the eternal God.

This book brings out these aspects and you will be delighted not only to read the blessed contents, but you will also begin to enjoy your fellowship with God and other believers as you personally and corporately delight in worshipping and praising the One and only Creator of the universe, to whom the Jesus Christ said, He seeks worshippers to worship Him in Spirit and in truth. This book is not just to be read and kept on the shelf; it must be shared with others. The lessons within it are a treasure. The Lord surely bless you as you delight to worship Him.

Rev. Ambrose Nyanga'u

Senior Pastor, Parklands Baptist Church

Endorsements

This is a good practical book on worship. It challenges both the worship leaders and believers to authentic worship that is really amiss in our day. The simplicity with which it's been written makes it easy to understand and brings clarity to the demands of a lifestyle of worship. If you want to enhance your worship experience, then this is a book worth reading.

Rev. Albert Shitakwa

Senior Pastor, The Green Pastures Tabernacle City Centre

Nairobi

Contents

PREFACE

In 1996 while at an annual conference at Nakuru Delieverence Church dubbed " Impact" the Lord spoke through a man and woman of God Rev.Allan and Eileen Vincent from USA . The words were as follows:" the Lord has appointed you to train true worshippers' to Him and has also put an anointing in your life to speak healing to women. I must confess that at that time none of the words made sense. I knew God had graciously given me the gift and talent of singing but honestly to be told that God wanted me (Leah) to train worshipper's for Him! Was incomprehensible!. The prophets immediately noticed the shock on my face and went on to assure me of God's guidance. I did just as Mary the mother of Jesus did and told the Lord to let that which he had spoken unto me be just as he had said.

In subsequent days after this 'shocking' experience something unusual happened. Let me pause here and qualify the shock. I was not shocked that I was asked to train worship, neither was it could not be done. So it was not shock born out of fear, but rather on who was commissioning the task-Jehovah himself! What an honour it was! I felt so privileged and in the same breath so unworthy and I could in a split second identify with the prophets of old Specifically Isaiah when he said ' Go away from me Lord, for I am man of unclean lips and live among unclean people'. There were moments that I doubted myself more than what was said. I wondered whether God really spoke it or the man of God just enjoyed the African worship and chose to express his delight! However, I knew him from the many years he had stopped by at Nakuru Deliverance church(Life Celebration centre), delivering God's word and I had also seen the manifestations of words of wisdom and Knowledge that God had given him. The Bible says 'You will know them by their fruit and for sure what he spoke always came to pass' But nothing I was experiencing supported this facts. I became sporadic in attending worship practice, interest to engage in corporate and individual worship went low , and truth be told, I always found something to occupy the worship practice sessions. It really became a battle just to create time. I used to wake up at 4 a.m and together with my Husband worship in low tones till dawn as we studied the word of God and express our awe of him. Soon that became unpalatable and had one excuse after another; from make believe backaches, to excuse of tiredness just to name but a few. It was at this point that I realised it is one thing to have the word of God spoken over me and another to be prepared to execute the purpose. I served God in several capacities in the worship teams but inside I really did not understand why the longing for More of God was becoming such an irresistible force. I asked God to help me.

As I matured in ministry I got my own portion of challenges. At first it didn't seem to bother me much as I understood the fruit of the spirit of bearing and forbearing with one another that That I hoped resided in believers and that they will soon discover they have drifted and would be apologising to me within no time. To my astonishment, I realised and began to identify with King David when he lamented . . . ."if it were my enemy who hurt me, I would understand, but it was you my friend, my brother whom we ate together" in one of the psalms he wrote.

Only then, did I realise that human beings are just human beings and that trials and tribulations are part of the packages that Christians of all walks of life go through and that it did not matter whether they were lay leaders, pastors, worship leaders or ordinary church members. I knew that one of my areas of growth was patience and God deliberately brought situations that tried my patience really hard. I may not have graduated from it yet but I have certainly grown.

As I observed and participated in worship I noticed a trend that was slowly fizzling out and another setting in. I found that there was a preference for upbeat, contemporary music as opposed to the classical, country music and g(old)en hymnals among other genres. This made me want to check out what it was about the songs that gave preference for one over another. I embarked on some informal research and it was amazing to note that a number of us sing for the sake of it. It is a song in fashion so why not go for it. To other's it was an identity issue that, if you belong to certain age bracket or live in certain contexts, you had to fit in otherwise you would be left out. In this regard therefore music and the choice became one aspect of exclusion and or inclusion, dividing rather than uniting. Yet to others it was a moment of a continuous discourse, why this and why not this. This book comes not to disqualify what we have held to be true or massage our choices but rather to shed light on what would biblically be acceptable worship.

In the initial chapters I take us through the Davidic tabernacle, basically looking at the historical background of Praise and worship. Looking at this historical background will then usher us to the distinction between Praise and worship though as we shall be seeing, there is an overlap sometimes and on other occasions they supplant each other.

In this book I have also attempted to introduce the concept of praise and worship from a communication point of view and have taken time to talk about what I have called the pre-requisites to effective praise and worship. It is amazing the response you get if you were to ask people to make a choice between good and evil and there is always a resounding yes for the good but when you ask further on what it takes to obtain the good, the journey suddenly begins to get bumpy. It is human nature to yearn and want excellent things however, for every good and excellent thing, there is a price to pay. Worship is a sacrifice and a heartfelt love affair. You are either in it or out of it. I have also talked about the barriers to an effective worship experience. This book can be a manual for all worshippers, pastors and any child of God who is hungry for more of God.

When properly done in genuineness, worship can be a weapon of warfare against the enemy. Paul and Silas demonstrated this well because as they sang, the bible records that the prison gates were opened, the chains were loosed and there was salvation for the jailer and his entire household. The three Hebrew boys as recorded in the book of Daniel i.e Shadrack, Meshack and Abednego praised God in the middle of a fiery furnace that had been heated seven times hotter than usual and the bible records that they came out whole and they did not even smell of fire. The children of Israel gave a shout and Jericho's walls tumbled down. What powerful weaponry we have in worship!

It is my prayer and hope that as you read this book, you will be energized by the spirit of God to desire to worship him in spirit and truth, because then and only then will you experience the delight of worship.

Blessings.

CHAPTER ONE

INTRODUCTION

When you think of Praise and Worship, What comes to your mind? Do you immediately picture yourself in church lifting up your hands and saying a few hallelujahs? Or do you see yourself in a closet with tears rolling down your cheeks and mumbling words that you can hardly understand? As for me, I picture these two scenarios and more. I see myself jumping in joy shouting at the top of my voice praising God for all he has done and for who He is. I see myself in a closet too overwhelmed by Gods presence and that can either bring tears to my eyes or make me remain quiet gazing upon his goodness and beauty, overtaken by his grace and mercies, and energized by his indomitable presence.

Praise and worship is an art that is not just learnt but can be passed on if properly entrenched into our Christian practice. Myles (2000) has emphasized that praise puts God in the first place. He went on to say that praise turns our attention from ourselves to God. This should therefore slow down some of us who think that their achievements have been due to their hard work, diligence, tenacity and sharp brains. This is not to say that there is no room for hard work and that we need to be like robots and wait for God to lift us, Absolutely Not!. In any case God himself in his Word has said that he will bless the work of our hands. The problem is with those of us who are not engaging our hands in anything so then how do we expect God to gate crash on our affairs and bless us? He says in Revelation 3:20,"I stand at the door and knock, if any man hears me and opens the door I will come in and dine with him and him together with me." Therefore He comes in as a gentle man on invitation.

This reminds me of when I was a student at Aldai girls' primary in Kapsabet one of prominent schools in the Nandi county. Whenever the then head of state President Daniel Toroitich arap Moi would visit, we would sing our hearts out to him praising him for what he had done and the fact that he could find time within his tight schedule as it were, just to stop by and see us. As a result of these praises, he would give us presents, like, financial gifts towards building a home science room or sometimes he would give us food that would last us a month or so. Praise elicits some actions from the one praised.

Praise is a warm expression of approval or admiration. It is a function of our will and therefore We are not coerced If by praising the second president of Kenya, led him to do some acts of kindness, how much more will our heavenly Father, the author of everything admirable and the creator of all things be moved toward us?. However, it may seem from the statement above that we praise God so that he can bless us, but not exactly so, we praise God out of hearts that are admiring his good works, appreciating his acts of kindness around us even before we can expect to get more. This therefore means that when one is not purposed to do it, then if they do it they are not doing it at will, therefore making the whole experience a dramaturgy, therefore not meaningful. Is there anything we can learn from great worship of old like the time of Moses, Solomon, David, and the times of the apostles? Yes! I definitely know that there is immense knowledge to be gained in looking at the historical background of praise and worship.

Historical Background of Praise and Worship

The largest book in the Bible is a song book (Psalms). Some of the greatest song writers in the Bible are our brothers Moses, David , Solomon and our sisters Miriam and Mary (the mother of Jesus). So you find songs sprinkled throughout Scripture from the Creation story to the book of Revelation. During Moses's time corporate worship was more prevalent than individual or private worship. We will look into the difference between the two later. The corporate worship involved all the children of Israel and the worship progressed in such a way that there was outer court worship, the holy place worship and then the holy of holies worship. Worship that took place in the outer court was preparatory to the worship that took place in the Holy place and the holy of holies.

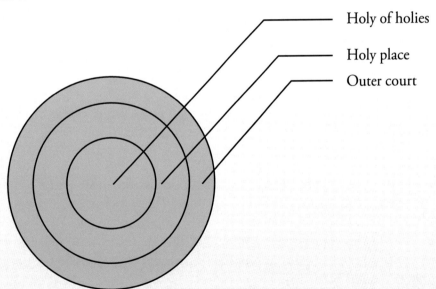

Holy of holies

Holy place

Outer court

Songs done in the *outer court* were meant to prepare the worshipper for the next level of worship which was entering the holy place. Songs at this stage focused more on what God had done, the many victories He had granted the children of Israel and the provisions he had constantly given them(Exodus 15: 1ff). The *second phase* was the holy place in this point the worshipper began to focus on who God is rather than what he had done. Songs at this point were no longer songs about God but rather songs to God. The children of Israel began to address God as He is. The *third phase* followed where they swam in complete admiration and awe of God. From the model of Moses worship is not just a song service it is a journey that takes into account the lifestyle of a believer and culminates in a celebration of God. The worship was based on law and rituals e.g they had to physically take a bath before they could ascend the mountain of God. Priests offered sacrifices on behalf of the people because men were not allowed in to the holy of holies (Exodus 30: 17-21).

Davidic Tabernacle.

Unlike Mosaic worship, that had a designated place of worship (temple), David's captures another dimension of worship. For King David, worship was a lifestyle. For David worship was not in any particular place. He praised God while he watched over his Fathers sheep, praised God and worshipped him when he was in great danger as he faced up with enemies of his flock (bear and Lion) and when he was happy over Gods victories for the children of Israel. Sometimes his skilful playing of the harp relieved King Saul from the torment of an evil spirit (1 Samuel 16: 23). He however had three key assistant that the Bible calls skilled musicians. These were: Asaph, Heman and Jeduthun. These three were set apart for the ministry of prophesying accompanied by harps, lyres and cymbals (1 chron.15:1).

They had 24 sons whom they trained in music and each of these sons trained, 12 members of their families totalling to 288.Another 4000 priests worshipped the Lord day and night.

There were still sacrifices being offered but the emphasis was on worship, praise and prophesying with the accompaniment musical instruments. The Ark of the Covenant was in full view of the people and anyone could enter.

Song progression for King David's tabernacle takes more or less the same pattern as that of Moses and Solomon in that the outer court was songs about God, then in the inner court, it was songs to God and the third phase was full of awe for God(1 Samuel 6: 14). The outer court involved upbeat songs that made the King dance to the point that his royal garments were torn, this made his wife Michal annoyed and resentful towards David but the King gave her a very appropriate answer that it was not to her but to God that he was rejoicing for victories.(2 Samuel 6: 20-23).

NEW TESTAMENT WORSHIP (JOHN 4:7 FF)

Many people in the New Testament stand out when New Testament worship is mentioned. I think of Jesus himself who sang and praised God together with His disciples. I think of Paul and Silas in Acts 16:24-30, who burst into song when they were thrown into prison and they sang their hearts out until the prison gates split open and salvation was attained for the jailer and his entire family. I think of Mary the mother of Christ who sang a song when she accepted the prophetic words spoken over her life that she was going to be blessed among all women and that she would also will be the mother of God's son.(Luke 1: 46ff)

Above all, I think of the Samaritan woman's encounter with Jesus in (John 4:19ff) and this is Where I dwell for a while. The woman of Samaria came to draw water from the well at the most unlikely time of the day at noon. Jesus sat at the well and asked her for water. By looking at the features of Jesus, she would have been able to tell that he was definitely not a Samaritan and so therefore he did not qualify to be given water by a Samaritan woman. After the encounter Jesus said to her. "If you knew the gift of God and who it is that asks you for a drink, you would have asked him and he would have given you living water". The conversation goes on to a point where Jesus asks the woman to go and call her husband. She candidly responded that she had no husband and Christ immediately applauds her for her honesty and begins to unveil her secret life before her very own eyes. Upon realising this, this woman says, "I perceive you are a prophet". From this point the conversation shifts in a different direction away from water and onto places of worship. Christ then tells her a very key statement that, "a time was coming and had already come that the true worshippers of God would worship God in spirit and Truth". This conversation between Jesus and the woman of Samaria changed the whole idea of where it is appropriate to worship God, the time and with whom. It is clear from this encounter that worship is a lifestyle and is done whenever and wherever, not necessarily on the mountains or even Jerusalem or better still not even in churches alone but whenever and wherever as long as the motive and intentions are pure.

Notice, Christ talks of a worshipper who should do it in spirit and truth. It is the matter of the heart. Therefore worship or even praise is judged by our hearts, why are we doing it and for what purpose? What do we want to get out of it? When we sing what is it that we want to display, is it to display the latest song genre and styles? Is it the latest twist of tonal variations? Are you trying to prove something to someone or all? Bottom line, I ask, what is your motivation? Under what or whose inspiration are you operating when you set out to praise and worship?.. Even before we delve in the motivation bit, it is paramount that we ask ourselves, what worship is. Therefore, what is worship? And what is praise? Is there any difference? Why do we need to pay attention to how we do the corporate worship? For this and more, walk with me through this next phase.

DISTINGUISHING PRAISE AND WORSHIP

Praise has been defined as a warm expression of admiration or approval. This has to do a lot with deeds that one has done in the past. It is like counting the happenings in terms of another's actions or deeds of kindness for another. When we praise God we recount what he has done not only in the past but also what he is doing in the present and in the future. Why? This is because God does not change the Bible says He is the same yesterday, today and forever. What He promised then He did and still does, for as many generations as are called by His name. We also praise God for who He is to us and not necessarily for what He has done. Everything that has breath according to the psalmist is to Praise God. Worship on the other hand according to Warren Wiersbe in his book, real worship is a total loving response to all that God is, says and does. It is looking away from us and to God. In terms of song delivery, praise songs are fast, energetic while worship songs are generally slow and not vigorous. We can praise men but worship is exclusively for God. Praise is always seen and heard but worship is not always heard sometimes it is quiet. Another difference is that praise involves shouting, jumping, clapping and vigorous dance, while worship calls for meditation. Allow me at this juncture to get deeper into these two i.e praise and worship.

Chapter Summary

This chapter focused on the introduction, the need for studying the subject from a communication point of view and also looked at the historical background of Worship. In looking at the Mosaic tabernacle one is left with the impression that worship was done in levels thus the outer court, the holy place and holy of holies where the priests were the only ones mandated to do so. Emphasize was also placed on the rituals, such as taking a bath before appearing in the presence of God. Today by the virtue of the shed blood of Jesus we have access to the throne room of Heaven and the invitation is come just as you are.

This chapter also looked a little bit at the worship in the New Testament with the key scripture being John 4vs 23, where Jesus encounters the Samaritan woman and details are expounded here. There is also a distinction between praise which the author has alluded to as the expression of admiration and great recounting of works done. When believers praise God, they tell of his wonderful works but also praise Him for who He is. Worship on the other hand is ascribing to God the glory, honour and worth due Him. It is intimate and there is no two way about it. You are either intimate with God or not at all. Worship is exclusive for God whereas in Praises we can even praise man. One can miss God in Praise but not in Worship.

CHAPTER TWO

PRAISE

Praise is a warm expression of approval or admiration. It is a function of our will, our own volition. In the Bible the tribe of JUDAH means praise. Praising God is looking at God in admiration. Going back to my experience at Aldai girls where we praised the second President of Kenya His Excellency Moi. All we ever sang about was what he had done for all the Kenyan school going children, by providing free milk famously known as 'Nyayo milk", celebrated the public service vehicles he had provided dubbed 'Nyayo bus service' just to name but a few. These praises motivated him to reach into his pockets and give us money for food and educational trips and sometimes pay for needy children's fees. Our praises to him were not in any way pegged on getting something from him even though we knew he was capable, but was rather our gratitude to him for what we understood to have come to us under his leadership as the President. In the same manner consequently, we praise God not because of what we expect him to do but rather for what he has done and is continually doing.

We praise God because he is Omnibenevolent (all loving). One of the biggest Christian challenges is to love people who we would consider unlovable. But as for our God he is all loving and even when we have fallen short of His glory and ashamed him by our actions, He still says,

> "Come to me all you that labor and are heavy laden and i will give you rest. Take my yoke and learn from me for i am meek. For my yoke is easy and burden light and you will find rest for your souls" (Matthew 11: 28ff)

When we praise Him, we dedicate ourselves to God's values, and to God's purpose

All humans have a duty to praise God and give him thanks (www.saintaquinas.com)

WHY SHOULD WE PRAISE GOD

- ❖ It is a good to praise the Lord (psalms 92:1). The Psalmist understood that praising God was pleasurable; proclaiming his love in the morning and his faithfulness at night, for God makes people glad. He goes on to marvel at the greatness of God and wonders in verse 5 'how great are your works, Lord, how profound your thoughts'.

- God is enthroned in the praises of his people. He inhabits our praises (psalms 22:3). One of the easiest and surest way of finding God is in the presence of His people, when they that are called by his name gather to exalt his name, praise him for who he is and what he has done, to celebrate the help that comes by the holy spirit of God and to appreciate the cleansing that comes by the shed blood of Jesus Christ cleansing us from all unrighteousness, makes praise awesome. Just knowing that we are no longer under any condemnation for we are now the redeemed of the Lord, makes the hearts melt in adoration and admiration for the Love of our Lives-Jesus Christ our Lord and saviour.

- There is power in praise e.g (Paul& Silas, Shadrack, Meshack and Abednego). Their prayers were answered only by lifting Jesus. One of the ways we do this is when we praise God. Can you imagine if Paul and Silas had tried to reason out their positions with the opponents? Could anything have been achieved? Do you think they would have been gladly released for their rationale for preaching Jesus? I don't think so. There are situations in our lives where confrontation and reasoning is relevant but there are other situations where trying to reason with the oppressors is not only inappropriate but disastrous.

- He is worthy of praise (Psalms150,68;8). He deserves all our praises and when we realise this fact, then we know we are not doing God a favour by praising him but on the contrary we do ourselves a huge favour when we praise the one that deserves it All.

- We praise Him because we were created to praise him (1 Peter 2: 9)

WHEN AND WHERE SHOULD WE PRAISE

We should praise God at all times in all manner of situations and places. Psalms 26:8-12, 34:1,113:22, 27:4(in buildings, while we go about our usual day to day activities, with other believers, alone, when we are happy and when we are not so happy to name but a few).

Praise is therefore vocal, exuberant, exciting and energetic BUT ALSO a continuous sacrifice. While preaching at the Green Pastures Tabernacle in Kenya, Rev. Russell Chipoyera of Zimbabwe applauded Isaac of the Bible for not disturbing his father when he was being prepared as a sacrifice that the Lord God had asked of Abraham. He did not complain at all even though he had enquired where the sacrifice would come from having noticed that they were already at the mountain of God and there was no sign of a sacrificial lamb. He lay there ready to be offered. The problem with most of us believers is that we jump off the altar table when things are not in the style we like. When we feel the songs are reaping off our pride we tend to hold onto what we consider important to ourselves and we are not bothered much with what God wants of us. We want to praise God decently and in a gentlemanly manner therefore putting us in good company with Mrs. Michal David. Queen Michal wanted her husband—King David to praise God in a certain demeanour one that would be considered acceptable before the dignitaries and "people of honor" during his time. Her husband praising God to the extent that his clothing became torn was not just humiliation to her as an individual but also to her dignity (in her portfolio as the queen). It is no wonder we don't experience God as we should because we are still not ready to be living sacrifices. We keep jumping off the altar instead of letting the owner of the incense to consume us making and moulding us to his own image as He so pleases, because if anything we are meant for his glory.

WHY PRAISE IS A SACRIFICE

Once we die to sin and are alive to God, we not only crucify our sinful nature but are raised to reign with Christ. In other words we no longer live for ourselves but in and for Christ Jesus hence mortifying the desires and longings of our sinful nature and instead replacing them with the desires and longing for God's own pleasure. We begin a new reality (no longer do we live for ourselves, but for the very one who gives us life, breath and everything else (Gal 2:20)

Sacrifice entails giving up something important to us e.g. time, energy, physical possessions, emotional attachments and even spiritual gifts. It is also a sacrifice of self (Romans 12:1), a holy life is one of the requirements (1Corinthians 6:19) that often call for a resisting of gratification of the sinful desires, constantly beating up ourselves to obey God in spite of the pressing demands of our human nature to want to drift etc.

One of the ways we sacrifice to God is by sacrificing ourselves for our brethren and those around us.

- ❖ Do not forget to fellowship(Hebrews 13:16). In this day and age where we get preaching from so many sources, books, Tevelision, God channels, radio, it is so easy to feel justified to just watch Spiritual channels at home and be contented. But the scripture warns us against that and says we should not give up meeting as some are in the habit. When believers get together some anointing is released corporately. It is also true that from hearing what God is doing in the lives of others challenges another person going through similar situation. Gathering together is both a social but spiritual nourishment that must not be neglected in spite of the blessedness of the times(the ability to get preaching from a myriad of ways)

- ❖ Pure religion is looking after orphans/widows in their distress. Someimes is bufffles me how easy we can be caught up in seasonal friendship and empathy of then widow and orphans immediately the man of the house passes on. Three weeks later all the promises of 'we will be with you, just call on us anytime 'seem to have flown faster that when it was made. This reminds of me of some story that was told me recently. The story talks of the cry of some widows who after their husbands went to be with the Lord, most of the church responsibilities are handed over to them because 'they are free' such that when guests visits church, the persons to take care of the guests would be the widows. This is so sad knowing that they too need help, they now have to run their homes as husbands and wives, the fact that they have no one to go back home to cook for is not only disturbing and shameful. It is important to take care of the widows, love on them reach out to them. Taking advantage of their predicament is sin. How we treat them can affect our worship experience because God demands a kind of worship that is born of truth and spirit.

❖ Everyman shall receive his own reward according to his own labour 1cor 3:7-9

❖ Be steadfast, unmovable, always abounding in the work of the Lord (1 Corinthians 15:58)

❖ Do not burden anyone while you preach the good news 1Thessalonians 2:9

❖ Your love for the invisible God is shown through your love of the visible brethren.

Tehillah is a Hebrew word that reveals other reasons why our praise has to be a sacrifice. It means giving praise based on someone's attributes. Israelites praised God based on what he had done and who he was to them. God's attributes include: Faithfulness, Compassion, Justice, Grace. Psalms 145 is a Tehillah chapter.

WORSHIP

Worship is an intimate conversation between God and Man. It is a lifetime of sacrificing to God what He requires. It is the ability to magnify God with all our hearts, spirit and souls. It is the response of God's Spirit to ours and can be said to be extreme obedience to God.

In the OT it is portrayed as an act of paying homage and devotion to God. It always took place at certain times and places. Jerusalem was the centre of Jewish worship (John 4; 20).Daniel prayed facing Jerusalem (Daniel 6:10) even though he was far from his home area.

Acts of worship are associated with altars (2kings 18:22, Isaiah 36:7) and gates (Jeremiah 7:2)

Disadvantage of this kind of worship is that it naturally tended to legalism-therefore it became so ritualistic that people missed the true essence of humility before God, love for one another and a holy life (Micah 6:8)

One may wonder at this juncture what worship really is. Some have said that worship refers to certain religious activities like going to church every Sunday or Saturday, paying tithes, offerings and sometimes giving other extras that have been called the 'love offerings' by some churches and ministers, others think of worship in terms of partaking of the Lord's table, singing hymns, choruses, listening to inspiring sermons and basically going through the church rituals. But what is worship really? And why does Jesus talk of True worship? (John 4: 23ff)

What is true Worship?

The English word worship or worth ship means to attribute worth or to ascribe to supreme worth. Therefore we render to God glory, praise and honour that is due to him. It is removing oneself from the picture and putting God first.

In the Greek Bible to worship is translated *Proskunein*. This is a compound of a verb with *pros* meaning coming towards and *kinein* meaning to *kiss*. It is also translated to mean kissing the feet of or prostration.

Other terminology for worship is the Hebrew word *abad/Latreuo* which refers to man's duty in the Garden of Eden which was to till the land (Gen 2:15) It is translated as *serve* and I guess this is where we get the aspect of worship service from (Revelation 22:1-5)

The other terminology for worship is prayer rendered denoted by the word tepillah/proseuchomai. This is usually because of an attitude of total dependence on God. Charles Spurgeon the great English teacher and preacher once said, **"You can tell how popular the church is by the attendance on Sunday morning. You can tell how popular the speaker is by the attendance Sunday night. But, you can tell how popular Jesus is by the attendance at the prayer meeting"**{ what would happen if our bosses called for a 7 o'clock meeting, would we dare give an excuse?} How come we find it so comfortable to come to a worship service whatever time we see fit? Imagine how unpopular Jesus is and has become in our services? So sad to say we love him and are not available for Him .But worship is not simply asking but dwelling in his presence.

A writer of *In pursuit of open heavens* defines worship as that ability to sacrifice to God what is wholly his. It is a moment dedicated to God and Him alone! It is never a time to start binding demons or devils because at this time one has come to a level of total admiration of the creator and what he is able to do and just a total surrender to Him and none other. No amount of distractions from the enemy can penetrate that intimacy. Therefore instead of binding the devils, just relax, love on the greatest love of your life the Lord Jesus Christ and the blessed trinity. Worship is not even a feeling but a declaration of who He is regardless of our state.

In the NT, Jesus reveals a dispensational change in the mode of worship(John 4:7-21).Jesus indicated that the time had come when there would no longer be any special place or time for worship since God is spirit and is omnipresent, He can be worshipped anywhere and anytime.

Worship is not a matter of outward action but a spirit to spirit devotion to God. We worship from our spirit it is like or similar to when we speak with tongues where our spirits pray while our mouths speak. We worship from our spirits but there is always an outward response. I like the definition by Warren Wiersbe when He writes, "Worship is the believer's response of all that he is—mind, emotions, will, and body—to all that God is and says and does". True worship must be felt it cannot be ritualistic. In the OT worship was associated to specific places and times that is why you find expressions of worship throughout scripture. Jacob erected an altar after an encounter with the tangible presence of God. True worship in both spirit and truth is far more than merely singing theologically correct songs in order to prepare our heart for the preaching and teaching of God's word.

I am convinced that what we call a good church service and what God would call a good church service can be two very different things. True worship can be noisy with celebration or quiet with intimacy. Psalm 46:10, says, "Be still and know that i am God, I will be exalted among the nations, I will be exalted in the earth." It is amazing how we talk about our Love for him. We should not be like Michal, Mrs. David who was dignified but barren. She got so offended by her husband who was fervent and passionate about the Lord's victory. Feel free to express yourself before the love of your life, the source of your every blessing, the Lord your salvation (Psalms 103 ff.)

WORSHIP IN SPIRIT AND TRUTH

In attempts to understand a worship that is done in spirit and truth, some have called it sincerity or doctrinal truth. Jesus Christ statement was a rebuke to both the Jews and Samaritans. He emphasized the truth to the Jews whose worship was outward and stressed the Truth to the Samaritans who did not know who they worshipped. Worship in spirit and truth means to sincerely worship the true God through Jesus Christ from our inner beings.

Worship is not for the purpose of obtaining anything from God, but giving to God. It is therefore the occupation of the heart not with its needs, or even its blessings but God Himself.

True worship is based on the Hebrew word "*Shacah*" which means to bow down in reverence, to prostrate oneself (Exodus 4: 13).Bowing is an attitude of submission and obedience. It involves giving ourselves unreservedly to God.

Aspects of Worship in Revelation

Adoration of God's being

Declaration of the Lambs worthiness

A Celebration of God's presence

Submission to His authority

Fearing and serving Him

The right attitude in worship begins with recognising God as the sole object of worship. A true worshipper will remain faithful to God even when God does not bless him or her. His or her submission to Christ is not based on rewards or punishments, but rather a solid relationship that is not based on God doing anything or nothing to the individual.

In practise, worship is a lifestyle of brokenness before God. Worship cannot be separated from service. Everything we do has to be for God's glory (Service, devotion, giving (Phil 4:18), acts of concern for others wellbeing (Rm14:8) and everyday lives (Denver Cheddie, 2001). Worship is a lifestyle and therefore not a onetime experience, you do not come to church to learn to worship but you come to corporately celebrate and worship God alongside other believers. Individuals who have a habit of worshipping God always have an easier time tapping into the tangible presence of God as opposed to one who has been an alien to God's presence throughout the week. The following are some of the expressions of worship.

EXPRESSIONS OF WORSHIP

- ❖ Cooperate singing-Psalms 68:4,2 Chron 5:13-14,Acts 16:16-34

- ❖ Singing in the spirit(tongues)

- ❖ Prophetic singing (Davidic Tabernacle)

- ❖ Prophetic playing e.g when King Saul was oppressed by an evil spirit, David played the harp and the spirit would leave. While the harpist was playing, the hand of the Lord came upon Elisha and he prophesied i.e 2kings 3:15

- ❖ Instrumental accompaniment psalms 81

- ❖ Antiphonal singing (dividing the congregation into two e.g in (psalms 136), where one group leads in a call and the other in response.

- ❖ Responsive singing (psalms 98)

- ❖ Raising of hands (psalms 134:2, psalms141:2, 1Tim 2:8 e.t.c).

- ❖ Clapping of hands (psalms 47:1)

- ❖ Dancing which does the following

  - • Releases joy (Ex 15:20) Miriam danced at the defeat of Egyptians

  - • Expresses community (Jer 31:13) Maidens, Youngman and old danced together

  - • Dramatic mime of the truth (Ezek 12:3-7)

- ❖ Bowing (psalms 66;23, Phil 2:10)

- ❖ Shouting (Psalms 100:1).

Having looked at the various aspects of worship from a historical background, worship in the old and New Testament one wonders then why talk of communicating through praise and worship? It looks like praise and worship is a heart to heart affair between God and man either corporately or privately. So where does the communication bit come in? Thank you for your critical thinking dear reader. I will explain this better if we first of all understand what communication is.

Communication as an essential element in Praise and Worship

Communication has been given diverse definitions. In fact it is like each book of communication has given its own definitions. What this means according to Infante, Rancer and Womack, (2003) is that people differ because they disagree on the nature of communication. But all in all the scholars do agree that communication takes place when the sender sends a message to a receiver using agreeable channels with a view to affecting the behaviour of the receiver therefore creating understanding. Communication occurs within a context. It is a planned endeavour so before communicating one takes time to plan what needs to be communicated, using what channels within what time period and what effects are expected. This reminds me of the times I used to teach that one does what we call the schemes of work, and lesson plans. These tools helped the teacher to know what text they will use, what illustrations to use, what channels to use, for instance: is it through the chalkboard, power point or audio—cassette and also there were provisions for feedback, a brief question answer five minutes before the end of a period. A teacher who planned and the one who did not plan are easily judged based on the flow of the lesson. It is the same way with public speakers; one that took time to plan has their ideas flowing whereas one that did not! Have their points mixed up so much so that even if they had the best of points, they would confuse the audiences until all is lost. It also presents a bad picture and lowers the credibility of the communicator. Corporate worship is better understood from the communicator's point of view and what he or she does before, during and after congregation worship is critical.

One communication scholar by the name of Lasswell came up with a communication model which I wish to use to illustrate my point. For Lasswel communication takes place in the following format. S-M-C-R-F where S stands for the sender who is usually the song leader or worship leader, M—for Message which is the content in the song choice, C—for the channel which is the voice and instrumentation, R-for recipients which are the congregation and F—for feedback. Which come in the responsorial singing, salvation, healing and all the fruit of the spirit. We will now look at each element and see how it works in praise and worship leadership especially the congregational type.

The communicator

This is the individual in the congregational worship who leads in a song or songs during the worship experience. Just like a skilful communicator would do, it is expected that the said worship leader takes time to plan for a worship experience. Planning would involve him or her studying the word of God, taking time in prayer, learning some musical instrument, challenging self to different styles of music, increasing their music repertoire and understanding the type of congregation she or he has to minister to. A worship leader must be creative enough in order to bring the beauty in a worship experience. I am a firm believer that God Has endowed us with gifts that if we improve on them we will be amazed on how effective we can be for His glory. Instead of having the same start off of the service, a worship leader needs to be aggressive to know what other ways can enhance the worship experience without being ritualistic and religious to the point of missing out on God. Other than changing the starting songs which many worship leaders do, one would choose appropriate scripture and the book of Psalms has it. For example Psalms 136 which has a call and response style. This way the worship leader or worship team can lead and the congregation can respond," For His love endures forever".

The art of reading should read with greater expression in an attempt to re-create the atmosphere of the event or the sense of conviction of the writer. This is because knowing that it is the inspired word of God, we should read it with authority, conviction and compassion. One of the ways that scripture reading can be made creative is by dramatizing some passages. By involving two or three readers taking character parts and the like. There is no harm in going an extra mile because God has made us creative being. From the days of the typewriter to date where we use emails is a clear indication that we are creative beings. So then why not use our creativity for God's glory?

Most communicators would begin their speeches with a quote, story or a joke. This art captures the minds of the audience to realise that life is real and also capture the mood of the hour. I find this lacking a lot in the worship leading, it is like in our subconscious we think of jokes, storytelling or quotes as unscriptural and therefore sin. Please whereas I know there is coarse joking that the bible warns us against there are some jokes that are good. I think we all need to take a leaf from Pastor Joel Osteen's model of creative sermon delivery in the USA always beginning with a joke to grasp people's attention and get them ready for the preaching of the word of God. I am not saying we all begin our sermons or songs with a joke or story but I am saying there is need to be creative as worship leaders because the audience who are the precious people in the congregation needs to capture the mood in the sanctuary and identify with our creative God.

Silence as an aspect of Worship

Hendricks one of the renowned worship writers talks about the *gentle art of silence* that seems to be missing in most of our corporate worship experience. We start by talking about God, then talking to him but hardly do we allow him to speak to us. We seem to be accustomed to sound so much so that we eschew anything that is contrary. We are so consumed with making "a joyful noise" to the extent of shutting out other elements crucial for a worship experience. It is as if there is suddenly a disconnect when there is some gentle silence setting. I have sometimes observed with dismay to see even the church leadership so afraid of silence to the extent that they behave inappropriately. Let me pause here and give you an example of a service I once attended. As I made my way through this church service, the worship leader was doing a great job and there was a heavy presence of the Lord, people were becoming slain in the spirit, eyes were wet with tears and people were literally enjoying themselves in God's presence; then something suddenly happened that left me baffled. I remember one lady standing up and walking towards the podium shouting "I am healed!". A handful of others were experiencing God differently, others were lying prostrate, others were sobbing with tears rolling down their cheeks and others in total admiration of God in silence. The Pastor then stepped up to the pulpit, grabbed the microphone from the worship leader and started an upbeat song. To be precise it was, "I will enter his gates with thanksgiving in my heart "In my mind I thought to myself, I thought we were already in His presence and experiencing the fruit of worship". Of course you don't have to guess what happened because as he led the song he got no response because the children of God were already enjoying God's presence. My question then has been, was the pastor sensitive enough to notice God's presence? The pastors must lead from the front in being sensitive to the spirit as well as being in charge of the service. I remember when we were dating (My Husband and I) there were times when we talked to each other until it almost became like a competition, then there were times when we sat in total silence and looked at each other in admiration. We still do this today. What I have noticed over the 15 years that we have been married, is that in those moments that we are quiet, we tend to appreciate each other more, but of course silence is preceded by some talk. I believe the scripture, "Be still and know that I am God" has not been fully applied in our services especially in the corporate worship because to others it is time to give announcements, to others it is time to release the Sunday school children, and still to others it is time to take offerings. There is nothing wrong with the church activities' that I have mentioned, they are part of our worship experience all I am saying is that the Father longs to minister to us even as we minister to Him.

We will now turn our attention to what a worship leader needs to know about the members of the congregation because these are really his or her audience. It has been said, the more you know someone the more comfortable you are around them. So what is the place of audience analysis to a worship leader?

AUDIENCE ANALYSIS

The worship leader as a communicator through song, dance, scripture exhortation etc also needs to know the composition of the congregation. Sometimes it helps just to know who you are ministering to. For example knowing the church doctrine and constitution for (those with a constitution) helps the leader to know how to communicate well through the songs. For example in the church that I grew up in, there was a lot of emphasis on hymnals as opposed to the contemporary hip hop, reggae music and the like. It is upon a leader from this background to go through the hymnals and know which songs fit in the talking about God and which ones fit in the talking to God. Praise and worship can be attained from whatever style of music for as long as the worship leader knows what goes into praise and what goes into worship. Knowledge of the congregation helps the worship leader to know the choice of songs and the congregational preference. By this I don't mean that there is no space for new things and styles to be learnt. Starting from the point of knowledge to the unknown becomes easier when the leader knows his or her audience. Some congregation would prefer hip hop style, others prefer country music, others a blend of the two, others whichever comes and so ministering to them becomes effective if we are able to minister to their needs even as we minister to God. Can you picture a scenario where English songs especially integrity music being sang in the rural Pokot, Marakwet or interior Garrissa where the language of communication is the native people's tribe only? Will a leader have achieved anything? Or better still will he or she be considered effective for ministering in Kiswahili to the Cream of society church where the members of parliament, cabinet ministers attend? Or will it be better to minister with English songs?

It all depends on the setting, so the worship leader must get to know who he or she is ministering to, if efficiency and effectiveness is to be attained. Most worship leaders have failed to lead people to worship God because of their failure to know their congregation. For example in a congregation that has largely old people from ages 60 and above it will be brutal to do hip hop songs and the vice versa is true.

Knowing how to communicate as a worship leader goes beyond the song selection, knowing the audience, further to knowledge of a musical instrument and understanding of some basics in music. It is prudent for a worship leader to at least learn one musical instrument but again knowledge of a musical instrument does not make one a worshipper, but it enhances the worship experience. A worshipper who knows their vocal ranges will know what range works well for a congregational singing as opposed to what helps them improve their vocal ranges in their individual voice lessons or trainings. What we are comfortable singing is not necessarily what the congregation will pick up and run with it. Knowledge of a musical instrument will help the worship leader practise so as to know what keys are appropriate for which songs and what keys are comfortable for all even if they are not music students. Having said that let us now focus our attention to the message.

Message

A message has been defined as the stimulus that the sender sends to the receiver. It can be verbal or non-verbal or both. The message for the worship leader or song leader for that matter is the content of the songs chosen for the worship experience. Someone once said, *"it is not what you say but how you say it that matters"*. I dare say in praise and worship songs, it is both what you sing and how you sing it. For example the Yahweh chorus that has been attacked for lack of flesh or content can be made to have content depending on how it is sang. For example one could sing the old fashioned:

Solo: Eeh Yahwehx6

All: Eeh Yahweh

Or better still dress it more in the following way . . .

Solo: Eeh yahwehx6

All; Eeh Yahweh

Solo: Mwanzo na mwisho, kimbilio, Jemedari wetu

(First and last, our refuge and our fortress)

All: Eeh Yahweh

Pastor John Wimber and Eddie Espinosa of Vineyard church in the USA prefer the song progression of (Psalms 95: 1-6) and I totally agree with them. According to Psalms 95 our praise and worship experience especially in a congregational singing follows this format but is not limited to it.

Come let us sing for joy to the Lord

Let us shout aloud to the Rock of our salvation

Let us come before him with thanksgiving and extol Him with music and song..

For the Lord is the great God and King above all gods

In His hands are the depths of the earth, and the mountain peaks belong to Him

The sea is His for he made it, and his hands formed the dry lands

Come, let us bow down in worship, let is kneel before the Lord our maker, for he is our God and we are the sheep of His pastures, the flock under His care.

Going back to the Mosaic tabernacle, the outer court would take up the first phase where the congregation enters his gates with thanksgiving and into the courts with praise. The progression of our worship should therefore be thanksgiving, praise and worship (which actually means worth ship of God).

A communicating worship leader will follow this progression carefully and with enthusiasm. David was also in agreement with this progression when he says in Psalms 100 enter his gates with thanksgiving, come into His courts with praise and later on says, lets us bow down before our God. The Lord's Prayer also captures this progression. It begins by saying Our father who art in heaven , hallowed be thy name, thy kingdom come . . . later on give us this day our daily bread and forgive us our trespasses as we forgive those who trespass against us . . . I have been in congregations that have begun with repenting before giving thanks and most often than not the worship experience turn out to be a flop. Jesus is well aware of our weaknesses and says 'come just as you are'. By repenting before giving thanks makes one fail to truly experience His cleansing because it is only when we see ourselves as he sees us that we begin to see our nakedness and begin to truly repent with the brokenness that comes by His presence. I also have been in worship experiences that once the progression was well done, the congregation began binding devils instead of loving on the Lord and just enjoying being in God's presence. I believe in the presence of God there is fullness of Joy and in His presence demons take to their heels if they have any. Let us now have a look at the channel component.

Channel

A channel is a means through which a message is conveyed from the source to the receiver. How a channel is used can either enhance or impede the communication process. For example voice is a channel that when used properly can pass information well. If in a congregation of one thousand members within a church there exists no public address system, then the people won't be receiving information appropriately due to the lack of audibility from several speakers. A worship leader who is soft can make the sound not be audible and what this means is that people will be straining their ears to hear and sometimes will perceive what has been said and sing the wrong word or phrases. When he or she is too loud also, it irritates the ears of the congregation. A skill must be put in place from the worship leader and sound men to make sure that the amplified sound is balanced not harsh to the ear nor faint to be heard.

Musical instruments too are channels that need to be used carefully so that the tone produced is within the key and audible enough. The tuning of the musical instrument should be done before the worship engagement to avoid unnecessary hitting of wrong keys in a bid to search for the right one. Our God is a God of excellence and must be served in a spirit of excellence.

Recipients'

The recipients' in the corporate worship set up are both God and the congregation. If a worship leader is one that condemns the congregation, the congregation will shield themselves and so the effects won't be achievable. The congregation can either receive or reject the ministry depending on the present ability of the worship leader and the entire worship team or if you like the backup team. A worship leader who starts by condemning people for singing as if they were dead or for clapping as if they don't want to, or sitting down when they are supposed to be standing does not only create a barrier to communication and worship but also hurts the very people he or she is supposed to take through a journey of experiencing God. Such worship ends up being a show off rather than a ministry.

Communication can be verbal or non-verbal. It could also come through our dress code as worship leaders. Is the way we dress appropriate for the group we are leading? Shall they be drawn closer to God or further? Please don't get me wrong, clothes do not determine how deeper you get with God as an individual because God who we are ministering to is not bothered, He knows the frame of man if you like, He knows your nakedness and so you are not exposing anything that He is not aware of. But the Scripture also challenges us to be salt to the people around us and to be careful not to make them stumble. Paul says if your eating meat causes your brother to stumble then do not eat for the sake of the brother. So I believe that if the dress code or language used is not appropriate for the audience we are reaching through the ministry of praise and worship, then I believe it is not only spiritual not to, but is also the right thing to do. Remember the goal of praise and worship is to take the congregation through a journey of experiencing God, to a point that they experience the fruit of worship as we shall be seeing later on. That is the very reason that I said earlier own that it is paramount that the communicator, who is the worship leader, should study his or her audience to know how to effectively communicate to them.

Feedback

This is the responsorial singing and the consequences of worshipping with the right attitude and as the bible says in truth and in spirit. One of the immediate results or feedback when we worship correctly, is that God comes to inhabit our praises and when He comes to a place, things are never the same. Salvation becomes a reality as people become convicted of sin, righteousness and the judgement to come. Healing also becomes evident as the Lord begins to heal the sick both emotionally and physically. Faith is also increased as people stay in God's presence.

Having said all these, is there anything then that must be put in place to ensure that an effective corporate praise and worship is attained? Yes! Let us now look at the pre-requisites of effective praise and worship

CHAPTER THREE

The Pre-requisites to an effective praise and Worship encounter

No man builds a house before first of all considering the cost, in terms of materials needed, human labour and the ability to cater for that cost. Proper planning makes the building exercise easy, because there is already a blue print. In the same manner effective leading is not the one hour or thirty minutes a worship leader spends leading praise and worship but rather, a lifestyle of total surrender to the Lordship of God. Our life outside church should reflect our surrendered life and so when we meet on Sunday or Saturday, it becomes a celebration of an already surrendered life. As worship leaders some of the things we should do include and are not limited to:

Prayer

One of the things that the disciples asked Jesus to do for them was to teach them how to pray. Isn't it amazing that they did not ask Jesus how to win many souls or ask for more power over the stubborn devils like those that refused to go and needed an intervention of prayer and fasting, but rather how to pray! I guess the reason the disciples asked Jesus for such a lesson is because they knew many ministries are birthed in prayer. Anointing to minister is also attained in prayer. I get amazed when worship leaders hardly attend prayer meetings and all they do is spend all the time singing.. I wished they would spend more time in prayer and the rest will fit in place. Abraham Lincoln the former USA president once said," if I had eight hours to chop a tree, I would spend six of them sharpening the axe" Lincoln understood that a sharp axe cuts faster and effectively. What happens today in the ministries we have in church is we take six hours reading how to present the sermon or how to sing within the key and only 15 minutes in prayer. It is no wonder the move of God in our services today has been limited and the church experience has been reduced to a display of talents rather than an edification of the church and her members. This is not to say that practice is not that important, it is of course but first things first. 2Corinthians 10 vs 3ff says," Though we are in the world, we do not wage war as the world does. For our weapons are not carnal but are mighty to the pulling down of strongholds" What demoted Satan from being the worship leader in heaven was his pride of wanting to be like God. Worship leading is one area of gifting that is a fertile ground for pride to germinate. This is because as one leads, people are drawn to initially the leading style and ultimately to the individual, so much so that the leader ends up being idolized. Before long if that individual does not lead worship for a Sunday or two, the attendance of the church begin to dwindle. If such an individual is not careful, he or she may begin to see himself or herself as equals with the servants of God in the house such as the senior pastors because I mean they too pull crowds. The only way to check on this is by constantly spending time in prayer so that the desires of the sinful nature are mortified. Consequently, the people coming to church are carrying heavy burdens that if you do not spend time in prayer, you may easily condemn a soul that needed a single word of encouragement to live on.

I cannot overemphasize the importance of prayer. Prayer must be done as a habit. It is a sweet smelling aroma before the Lord so keep on doing it.

Readership of the Word of God

In Jesus' temptation in the desert, he made it clear to Satan that,' man does not live by bread alone but by every word that proceeds from the mouth of God" The bible is a super book and cannot be equated to any other. This is because it is the only book that gives a believer an identity that is eternal. In a dark world, the word of God is a lamp unto our feet and a light unto our paths(Psalms 119 vs105). In reading the word of God a worship leader is able to minister properly to both God and man. Dr. Myles Munroe says that, 'worship is setting pressure on God" . Our God wants to hear us speak back to him. He loves to be told, 'You are the great I am, You are alpha and Omega, You are the greatest of all' and so on. By saying them back to him we set pressure on him to come and prove Himself strong on our behalf. You cannot set pressure on God if you do not read His word; to know who He truly is, for you to believe it and speak it back to him. Most of our songs today are devoid of God's Word and so they have dismal impact. But songs that capture the Word of God live long. Consider the great Hymns of old they still make sense today because they are word of God rich. Allow me to applaud the songs of integrity singers and our own Kenyan Gospel artists the late Angela Chibalonza and Reuben Kigame who have constantly sang songs that are Bible rich. There are so amny examples across the globe too for instance: Martha Munizzi, Hillsong, Ron Kenoly, Don Moen to mention just but a few. It is no wonder their songs are sang a lot in our worship services and I guess individual worship as well. As a gospel artist I have come to know the power of singing God's word back to God. In one of my albums I sang the song *Ibo kwongut wee Jehovah* which means you are great thou Jehovah I never thought of it to be any heat song because it did not have strong beats but today many people would request that this song be played on the local radio station KassFM. This is a Kalenjin radio station in Kenya. I challenge the worship leaders to compose Word rich songs that will be used in churches for worship. This will be a legacy that shall remain even after they are long gone.

Learning of a musical instrument

It is not mandatory to learn a musical instrument as a worship leader but it helps you to know when the musicians are giving you the right key or not. Notice it is not all the musicians who have mastery of musical keys. It also helps you during your own vocal training because you are able to enlarge you voice register.

Learning from others

This is the best way to learn and it can take on many forms. Jesus used this method to teach His disciples. If you have a good mentor in your church, watch them and learn from them. In this situation you can watch them in a weekly worship setting. Tell them that you are interested in learning, study what they do. Study what makes them successful and learn from their strengths and weaknesses.

If you're not blessed with a good mentor in your local church, search out a mentor. This can take many forms. You can go to worship conferences and watch the leaders and attend their classes. You can go to local worship events and watch leaders. You can attend other churches as the opportunity arises and note what each church does well (and not so well). You can also buy videos of worship leaders and note their different styles and ways of leading.

Chapter Summary

The chapter focused on the definitions of praise and worship and underscored the fact that worship is a lifestyle. Communication as an essential element of an effective praise and worship encounter is also underscored in this chapter. When a worship leader fails to know who his or her audiences are in the corporate worship experience then he or she is likely to miss the purpose of worshipping in the first place. Some pre-requisites to an effective praise and worship experience are also discussed here, among them being a surrendered life to the Lordship of Christ through readership of the word of God, vocal exercises and prayer among others.

CHAPTER THREE

SONG SELECTION/PROGRESSION

Song progression precedes song selection. Before a person starts on a journey they first consider whether they have enough bus fare or gasoline and whether the time to travel is sufficient. It is a process and even when one completes a journey it is not considered successful until they return to the place they set out from. Planning for the worship leader is of great importance. There are several types of sermons and it is only fitting for the worship leader and the pastor to work hand –in—hand. Services or worship experiences can either be thematic or spontaneous.

Thematic service

This is a type of service that the preacher literary shares his main text or focus for service with the worship leader. It is now upon the worship leader to come up with songs that reflect the text to be studied so that song reinforces what shall be preached. For example is the text of study is Isaiah 6: 1 ff and the focus is on Gods awesomeness, then the song leader comes up with songs that talk about God's awesomeness. The service could further be enhanced by having teams such as drama team act out a skit on God's awesomeness. The church could have some decorations depicting this attribute of God. This type of service is usually rich because if the church member arrives late and could not participate in the worship, he or she can get the message from the bulletin, the drama team or the decorations around the church on that particular service.

The only undercurrent of this kind of service is that it can be very ritualistic and requires that the pastor really spends time with God so as to know what God's heart beat is concerning the members of his flock.

The Spontaneous service

This is a kind of service that is not corporately planned by the pastor and the worship leader. Each one of them seeks God on their own and come up with songs and sermon for the day. The downside of this service is that should the man or woman of God not seek God in advance and neither did the worship leader , ministry to God and the people can be hard. The benefit is that each of the church leaders seem to seek God on their own therefore no lazing around expecting the other to do the seeking. Again because there are no restrictions on the theme or topic, there is liberty to worship however and whenever.

Whatever type of service it may be, a communicating worship leader needs to spent time with God. Munroe (2000) stated that, "Praise that reaches God takes beyond the confinement of routines, yet actually follows a pattern or a progression". I would like to propose a type of song progression that i find effective and easy to do. This is not to say that any other progression does not work. It is what works for me and has worked elsewhere. Psalm 95 gives the song progression in five distinct phases

Five Phases of a Worship Workout

Eddie Espinosa and John Wimber, pastor of The Vineyard, developed a five-phase pattern for their "worship set."

In their worship services, the choruses were short, and their worship set was long. Rather than singing songs in random order, they recognized the need to smoothly link the many choruses and provide a sense of progression.

They identified five different kinds of choruses and how they could be linked into a sequence. The five phases are (1) invitation, (2) engagement, (3) exaltation, (4) adoration, and (5) intimacy, with a summarizing closeout.

Espinosa finds scriptural support for the five-phase model in (NIV):

Invitation: "Let us sing for joy . . . shout aloud."

Engagement: "Let us come before him with thanksgiving."

Exaltation: "For the Lord is the great God . . . the mountain peaks belong to him."

Adoration: "Come, let us bow down . . . let us kneel."

Intimacy: "For we are the people of his pasture, the flock under his care."

1. You can also arrange your chorus and hymn repertoire into these phases. Here are some guiding principles: worship that has a goal and direction worship that respects the psychological dimension worship that reflects the character of God (both transcendence and intimacy) lyrics that point to function (singing "about" and later "to" God) mixing of hymns and choruses (richness, variety) smooth transitions (linking both pieces and phases) avoiding distractions (not "jumping around" but maintaining focus) common tempos common words common keys adequate preparation yet open to the leading of the Spirit

Let's look at each phase in more detail.

Invitation

The invitation phase is a call to worship. It accepts people where they are and begins to draw them into God's presence. Most people need to wake up, warm up, and be energized before they're ready for the spiritually strenuous work of true worship.

The usual feeling in the invitation phase is celebratory, upbeat, and praise oriented (but not necessarily so). It may be accompanied by hand clapping. The lyrics are directed to the people, not God, telling them what they are about to do.

The chorus "Don't You Know It's Time to Praise the Lord?" is a good example of an invitation song:

Notice how the lyric does the inviting and focusing without our having to resort to verbal scolding ("Can we have quiet!") or exhortation ("Put the worries of the world away and give attention to God"). The music can do that without the leader's having to lecture.

"The skillful leader woos the congregation into worship like the patient lover draws the beloved," says Paul Anderson, a Lutheran pastor in San Pedro, California.

For a vigorous call to worship with hand clapping, the Hebrew chorus "The Celebration Song" would be excellent, whereas a more mellow call could be "Let's Forget about ourselves and Magnify the Lord and Worship Him," or "Come, Worship the Lord."

Traditional churches could use hymns during this phase and conclude with a scriptural call to worship. In the invitation phase, the leaders continue until they have made contact with the people and everyone is focused. For example a chorus with these wordings, "from the rising of the sun to the setting of the same, the name of the Lord is to be praised"

The invitation phase is particularly helpful for churches meeting in high school gymnasiums or other structures where worship symbols such as a Communion table, an open Bible, stained glass windows, banners, or other visual worship enhancements are absent. The songs at this level help the audience to focus their attention to the purpose of gathering.

Engagement

In the engagement phase, people begin to turn their attention directly to God, not to one another. Often the lyrics are addressed specifically to God.

A good example of this kind of engagement is the song by Reuben Kigame

"Mshukuruni bwana, kwa kuwa yu mwema kwa maana fadhili zake ni za milele" which when translated means: Gives thanks to the Lord for he is good his love endures forever. (Psalms106: 1b)

A more contemporary song that can serve in the engagement phase is "I will enter His gates with thanksgiving in my heart . . . ."

Espinosa likens this phase to the engagement period before marriage, for the congregation is now attentive, serious, ready to fully focus on the wonderful attributes of the Beloved.

Exaltation

In the exaltation phase, the people sing to the Lord with power, giving meaningful expression to the lofty words of transcendence-words like great, majestic, worthy, reigns, Lord, and mountains.

Musically, we generally use greater pitch spans than in the other phases. The high notes bring out a dynamic response and project a sense of God's greatness. If the people stand throughout the invitation, engagement, and exaltation phases, their response will be stronger.

Traditionally, hymns like "All Hail the Power of Jesus' Name" and "Immortal, Invisible, God Only Wise" are examples of exaltation.

Contemporary songs like "Majesty" and "Our God Reigns" are also appropriate.

Adoration

In the adoration phase, people are usually seated though others prefer to keep standing. The dynamics gradually subside, the melody range may reduce to five or six notes, and the key words may be you, Jesus, and terms of personal worship and love, as in the chorus "We Worship and Adore You."

In the exaltation and adoration phases, two sides of God's character receive expression. Exaltation focuses on his transcendence (his wholly "Otherness"). The adoration phase focuses on his immanence (his closeness to us).

Intimacy

The last phase moves from immanence to intimacy. This is the quietest and most personal expression of worship, with God addressed in terms such as Abba. The choruses "In Moments Like These" and "O Lord, You're Beautiful" reflect the tone of this phase.

This is the "kiss" of worship. One meaning for the Greek word for worship, Proskuneo, is "to turn toward to kiss." Kissing requires closeness, which comes only if properly prepared for in the preceding phases.

While the lyrics in the exaltation phase may emphasize the corporate "we," in this phase they now take the personal dimension of "I," as in "Father, I Love You."

Sometimes it's a good idea to change the wording of familiar songs to make them fit this intimate phase. For instance, "we worship you" can change to "I worship you" in the lyric, "I worship you, almighty God, there is none like you."

"Him/his" can be changed to "you/your" in "It's so sweet to trust you, Jesus, just to take you at your word."

Musically, this usually means a softer mood. Percussion may not suit the intimacy phase.

The worship set ends when the people stand for a close-out chorus or hymn-" To God be the glory great things he hath done," for instance-that leads out of intimacy and helps people adjust to the next event in the service.

We don't want to stumble or break our stride while running. Overall, think of the tempos the following way: invitation and engagement (running), exaltation (jogging), adoration (walking), and intimacy (stopping, silent communion, gazing).

Chapter Summary

This chapter focused on song selection as a key element to effective communicating through praise and worship encounter. It also lays emphasize on the right progression based on the book of Psalms 95. It has also looked at the two types of worship which are the thematic worship (planned by both worship leader and the preacher) and the spontaneous where both the preacher and the worship leader seek God differently and wait to minister. The spontaneous worship can both be a recipe of missing out on God for lack of corporate anointing but can also cave a situation just in case one of the key ministers in the worship service missed out on God the other can rescue the situation. Thematic worship on the other hand can turn to legalism but if much time is taken by leaders, the service can be enriching and also planning for such service is easier.

The chapter has also attempted to give a simple worship work out as proposed by Espinosa a writer on worship of whom the writer has adopted his progression because it is supported by scripture.

CHAPTER FOUR

Benefits of having DELIGHTFUL praise and worship

As we praise and worship God, in the truth and spirit we experience His benefits which i call the fruit of worship. The key benefit of Praise and Worship is God's presence. The Bible says that in the presence of God there is fullness of Joy. Therefore as we worship him, The God who inhabits the praises of His people do come and take habitation in our midst.

It is within his presence that *Faith in our God begins to increase* and then needless to say is that we begin *to experience His loving kindness and compassion. Healing* of diseases happens and several miracles begin to take place. The greatest of all being the *salvation of souls*. This is because in the presence of God sinners are convicted of sin, righteousness and even the judgement to come. There is also the ministry of the word of knowledge and word of wisdom being experienced. Several prophetic utterances can be given and proclamations done under the influence of the Spirit of God. Answers to prayer are also evident for example if one person came in very down casted and trusting God to meet them at the point of their needs, then the Lord lifts the heaviness and gives them joy then we consider this to be an answer to prayer. Even as we speak of God's visitation, there are those hindrances that can prevent us from experiencing God as we should and consequently, missing out on the fruits of worship. Allow me to now turn your attention to these hindrances or barriers to effective praise and worship.

Barriers to experiencing delight in praise and worship

One of the key barriers to experiencing delight in Praise and Worship Includes:

1. The inability of the worship leader to connect with the people.

This can come in the form of the dressing, language usage and the tone of communication. If the worship leader has dressed in a provocative manner, the congregation won't flow in worship. On the other hand if the worship leader dressed in jeans to a mixed congregation it would not be appropriate but if the congregation were teenagers, dressing in jeans would be appropriate yet dressing in suits for this category would be considered inappropriate.

2. The lack of prayer in the individual worship leader as well as the congregation

A prayer less church is a powerless church. The more we pray the more we see our imperfections and the more we surrender to the Lordship of Christ. If one does not wait on God, it becomes very difficult to lead people before His presence, because you are a stranger to the presence as a leader. One can comfortably lead another to a place they have been. Having a prayer less worship leader is like an inexperienced driver on the road who has to park the car beside the road to engage another gear then return to the highway. Imagine the kind of torture that is especially if the passengers' were in a harry to catch up with some deals or assignments. To be an effective worship leader or pastor one must invest in prayers. Develop a discipline to constantly pray for indeed apart from God we can do nothing.

3. Lack of Studying of the word of God and living it

The entry of the word of God brings light to our lives so the Bible says. I wonder how much time to really consider the impact of God in our lives. If the word of God were to dwell in us richly, we would not be taking chunks of our time engaging in recipes from the world. I have been watching keenly on the unfolding trends in the church today where a bigger percentage of sermons preached are what one could get elsewhere. Topics such as managerial skills, how to handle stress, among many which have in turn become more motivational talk to the detriment of the richness of the Word of God to our situations. Whereas am not against people being helped through their besetting situations such as oppressions, depression and being challenged to take charge of their predicaments, i do believe that the central crust of our teachings and sermons should be based on the ever powerful word of the God. In fact the word of God has answers to all our life problems. To the weary the word of God says, come to me all ye that are weary and are heavy laden and i will give you rest. For my yoke is easy and burden light and you will find rest for your souls (scripture) To those that are worried about what tomorrow holds, the word of God comes to encourage them to cast all their cares to Him for he cares for them.(scripture).The fundamentals of our Faith should be reinforced even today. I am of a strong opinion that the word of God does not go out of fashion .It is the only constitution that does not need review. What he said year past is still valid today. No wonder the scripture says whatever God says is forever established. What happened to people being challenge to live right lives, pray without ceasing, being each other keepers, providing for the needs of the needy, celebrating the spiritual gifts and the like? Is the church loosing it? Are we changing our messages in order to be relevant to the society? If this be the case then i guess we need to make a quick about turn and return to our maker. Go back to the manual which is the word of God and draw our motivation from there only then can we live meaningful lives. Paul while exhausting believers once asked," what shall it profit a man if he gains the whole world and loose his life to eternal damnation?" Quite a reality check don't you think. A leader therefore needs to saturate his life with the word of God. David said, "i have hidden your word in my heart that i may not sin against you."

4. Too much lecturing as opposed to leading by grace

As a public speaking consultant , one of the things that determines a great speaker form a dull and dross one, is the way the choose their words and what kind of introductions as a matter of fact the first three sentences are critical to a public speaker it could either make or break. A great introduction is one that acknowledges the audience, states the purpose, establishes credibility of the speaker and sets a preview of how the presentation will flow. Though this is more academic in nature i believe the same applies to anyone with an information to relay in our case the worship leader has some content to share with others through song, dance, and other non-verbal cues such as clapping of hands, raising of the hands, facial expressions etc. I have also noticed and have attended corporate worship experiences that the worship leader has the audacity of talking at the congregation rather that talking to them. They go something like," You are so dull today you like that you didn't have breakfast, why are you staring at me begin to praise the Lord, some of you are praising as though a gun was put on your throats, come on praise like you know what you cane here for! Here i have sampled just a few of them.

Sometimes it could even go a nudge higher and the worship leader begin to really sound insensitive and will say words like," put those hands straight up, i see some of you still seated, i said stand up and raise your hands up, you are raising it to God and not Me. Come on am waiting . . ." If there are worship leaders that fits the description i just gave, i think it would be prudent for them to know that the work of worship expressions, be it hand lifting, lying prostrate, bowing down, clapping of hands is entirely the work of the spirit. People respond differently to the revelation of God's love in their lives differently and so there is no uniform way. I am not in any way saying, they should not be told to raise hands, but i am against the coercion that comes as though one was appointed a head boy or girl. The things of the spirit are spiritually designed. You will real.ise that when you are in tune with the spirit of God, and are lifting hands people are likely to follow suit, and when you are urged by the prompting of the spirit you do it in love and with courtesy. For example, may i kindly ask all of us to stand up, shall we rise up our hands and give God a hearty hand club etc.

Conclusions/Recommendations

Praise and worship is one key element of our congregational worship. For many days we as the church of Jesus Christ have trivialize worship by turning it to a receiving session. We go before our God with lists of the things we want him to do for us. For many of us the time of congregational worship has been turned into moments of a performance show depending on the latest trends in the world of music and styles. To others it is a moment to hook up with the coolest girls and young men in the worship team and still to others it is time to make up for the busy week away from the bible and brethrens. What we always forget is that God has a need and that need is that he always seeks people who can worship Him in spirit and in truth. Dr, Myles Munroe (2001) said if God would have a weakness, it would be for worship.

This book has also explored communication as an effective tool of ensuring that our spiritual connectivity is in tune to our delivery and that God enjoys creativity too. We need to think of ways that as worship leaders we study our congregations' to ascertain the kind of audience we have. This knowledge would serve as a basis unto which we select music and instrumentations' for congregational worship service. Some songs do well in other environments because communication is contextual and does really bad in other settings. My challenge to pastors and all the children of God is to serve the Lord with gladness but also with understanding. It is no wonder the bible ion Hosea 4:6 says that my people are destroyed for lack of knowledge. We can only tap into the immense intensity of God's visitation if we take into consideration the pre-requisites to effective praise and worship. Areas of further research include the life of a worship leader or Music director and also the appropriateness of some music genres in specific congregations'. Have fun p[raising and worshipping your saviour and creator. Remember you were created to worship Him.

Chapter Summary

This chapter focused on the benefits of effective praise and worship such as the manifest presence of God and the ministration of the spirit of God in diverse works such as healing the sick, salvation to the unsaved, among other benefits and also put across the aspect of planning prior to the experiences in the worship service. It also looked at some of the hindrances' of effective praise and worship among them , the prayerlessness of the worship leaders, lack of proper study of the congregation, poor song selection and progression and stage presentations. The chapter has also indicated areas of further study such as the capacity building of worship teams, the life of a worship leader etc.

Thank you and have a delight in worship. AMEN.

Printed in the United States
By Bookmasters